Dewdrops, let me cleanse
in your brief, sweet waters
these dark hands of life.
Basho
1644-1694 A.D.

Of all things most yielding

What is of all things most yielding

. . .

Can overcome that which is most hard,

. . .

Being substanceless, it can enter in
even where there is no crevice.
That is how I know the value
of action which is actionless.

. . .

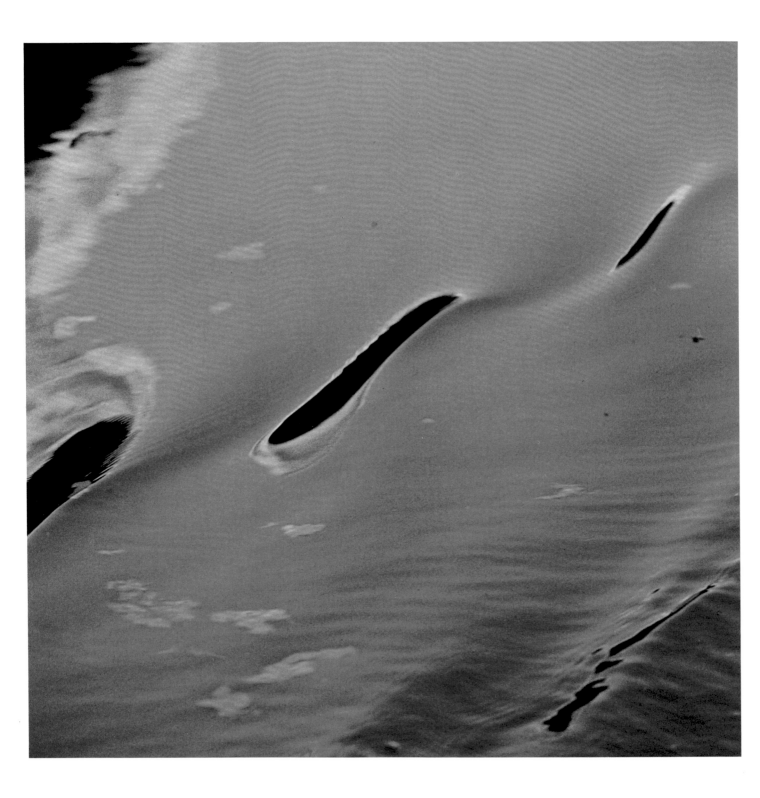

But that there can be teaching without words,
Value in action which is actionless
Few indeed can understand.

LAO TZU
5TH CENTURY B.C.

There is nothing
which heaven does not
cover,
and nothing which earth
does not
sustain
CHUANG TZU
369-286 B.C.

Of all things most yielding

PHOTOGRAPHS BY JOHN CHANG McCURDY

SELECTIONS FROM ORIENTAL LITERATURE BY MARC LAPPÉ

Edited, with a foreword by David R. Brower

FRIENDS OF THE EARTH ◉ SAN FRANCISCO · NEW YORK · LONDON · PARIS

McGRAW-HILL BOOK COMPANY NEW YORK · ST. LOUIS · SAN FRANCISCO · TORONTO

Foreword

The nation shattered, hills and streams remain.
A city in spring, grass and trees deep:
feeling the times, flowers draw tears; . . .

TU FU
713-770 A.D.

HILLS AND STREAMS *indeed remained in* 1950, *but it was rubble that was deep in a city in North Korean spring when American bombs buried a ten-year-old boy they had just made an orphan. Expecting never to be found and dreading a lingering death, Chang tried to kill himself the only way he could think of that the rubble would let him—by reaching his fingers into his brain through his eyes—and he tried hard enough to make bruises that still show faintly. Then he heard his grandfather calling him, responded, and was rescued. For a while he supported himself by shining G.I. shoes, and earned enough extra after some ten thousand boots to buy "a box camera that worked sometimes." In* 1958 *he found himself in Berkeley, with his first name translated to John and a new last name, that of Mr. and Mrs. Richard McCurdy, who had adopted him.*

He worked for his Bachelor of Arts degree in Design and Arts, with emphasis in photographs, film, and creative writing at San Francisco State College. Early in the 'sixties, he brought a selection of his photographs to the Sierra Club office in San Francisco, where Robert Golden was deeply impressed and persuaded him to leave them for a while. It became quickly clear that the eyes that had miraculously been spared had a most extraordinary way of seeing. But before anyone could quite determine how the photographs could be published, Mr. McCurdy was off to Uppsala University as a graduate student in the California State Colleges International Programs, where he worked on exhibitions and experimental films, and prepared illustrated articles for publication in Sweden, Denmark, and Holland. In 1970 *he became head of the Photography Department at the Kursverksamheten, Uppsala University.*

Friends of the Earth was now well into its publishing program, and I was happy to discover Mr. McCurdy's whereabouts. His camera had become a musical instrument and his seeing was in no way diminished. His wanderings with camera had taken him from the outskirts of San Francisco on to the last days of Glen Canyon (now drowned by Lake Powell), down into Mexico, then into the various Scandinavian countries, Iceland, Southern Europe, the Middle East, and northern Africa. We have avoided saying which photograph was where because we think what, not where, counts most.

He has not got to China yet, and it may seem a bit bold to rely almost wholly upon Chinese literature for the theme and melody that accompany his work. But somehow they are beautifully apposite, perhaps because of the spareness and honesty of both. Marc Lappé thinks there is a certain Eastern quality to the photographs, hastening to add that he knows no more what Eastern is than anyone who is Western-reared and bound by culture to a Western way of seeing. As he says, the photographs are peculiarly able to penetrate one's mind and to stay there a long time. Mr. Lappé's selections from Oriental literature do the same thing.

Marc Lappé was born in New Jersey in 1943 *and is now Associate for the Biological Sciences at the Institute of Society, Ethics, and the Life Sciences, Hastings-on-Hudson, New York. His undergraduate and graduate work at Wesleyan University, where he majored in biology and pathology, included Eastern studies; his Ph.D. program at the University of Washington combined experimental pathology and Eastern philosophy. He was enthralling small audiences with details about acupuncture some time ago.*

With Mr. Lappé's approval, interludes have been added from the late Henry H. Hart's The Hundred Names *and its illustrative translations of Chinese poetry spanning four millenia. "Nature in its alternating seasons, in its changeable and varying moods," Mr. Hart wrote, "is unceasingly immanent in Chinese life . . . evident at every turn in Chinese verse." The keenness of observing blossoms and trees, warmth and melancholy, pools and rain, the wild goose winging, he said, is in the songs of the sons of Han, from Confucius to the Republican revolution. But neither more nor less important than rocks, trees, waters, or dragonflies is man. And love pervades the beauty of the verse, just as it does the photographs.*

Much is to be learned, in parts of the world that have trouble living four hundred days or weeks in peace, from China, where, however little the leisure for the arts of peace, however hungry for plunder and ease the Tartar hordes of the north were, the people managed to live four consecutive centuries without war. They did less damage to the land in four millenia than we seem easily to have brought about in a single century.

There are probably many reasons for this difference, but three loom. Until the 1920 *census, China had not reached a popula-*

tion of three hundred million people for its vast space. Although that number has now grown enormously, today's several hundred millions use less electricity for all purposes than the United States uses for air conditioning alone, and the U.S. is two hundred fifty times more demanding of energy for its wet-rice culture than is China. The several hundred electrical slaves each of us enjoys in the U.S. not only pollute freely but also give us the power to tear the land mechanism apart; perhaps they also teach us ignorance of detail and contempt for how the land works, and the importance of it. These are attributes China does not seem to have achieved.

Of all things most yielding *can remind us that for all this lack of achievement, China has somehow been civilized for a* long time. We can be too, if we can somehow look about us and note that it is possible for nations to survive without being second to none—that it is even necessary for most nations to be something besides number one, and possible even then to hold onto important liberties. No one will be civilized much longer unless all the peoples who are now tearing voraciously at the planet they overcrowd and overstress learn swiftly to believe that it is the only one, and let their actions be informed accordingly, toward it and toward each other. Each can start at home, celebrating an earth that is still beautiful.

DAVID R. BROWER
President, Friends of the Earth

Never in this world does hatred cease by hatred;
hatred ceases by love, and this according to a law
which has existed forever.
NOBLE DOCTRINE OF GREAT COUNCIL OF BUDDHISM
20TH CENTURY

Of all the elements, the Sage should take Water as his preceptor.
Water is yielding but all-conquering. Water extinguishes Fire,
or, finding itself likely to be defeated, escapes as steam and re-forms.
Water washes away soft Earth, or, when confronted by rocks, seeks a way round.
Water corrodes Iron till it crumbles to dust; it saturates the atmosphere
so that Wind dies. Water gives way to obstacles with deceptive humility,
for no power can prevent it following its destined course to the sea.
Water conquers by yielding; it never attacks but always wins the last battle.
The Sage who makes himself as Water is distinguished for his humility;
he embraces passivity, acts from non-action and conquers the world.

TAO CHENG
11TH CENTURY A.D.

Introduction

"How are we to understand this life?" asks the initiate.

"All things are interconnected," replies the sage, "and interpenetrate each other as one."

WHAT IS THERE that makes this kind of dialogue so pithy yet so impenetrable to our Western minds? A war correspondent in Vietnam encountered this dilemma when he asked his North Vietnamese host to explain the difference between the principal contenders for political dominance at that time, Bao Dai and Ho Chi Minh. His host said, "If you are to understand these two men, you must understand this: Bao Dai is a heavy, corpulent person. He is like water—yielding, yet inclined to fill the places left by others before moving to new ones. But Uncle Ho is lithe and wiry. He is like fire, ready to burst forth at the first opportunity."

"Does this mean," the correspondent asked, "that Ho will oust Bao Dai soon?"

The host answered, "Not necessarily. If one wishes to overcome water, he must not oppose its nature: it must first be left to seek its own level."

Do the Vietnamese really believe that human qualities can be described and human actions predicted purely by analogy to nature? Would not this lead to a complete loss of human morality? In a classic exchange, two Chinese thinkers touch on this question:

Kao Tzu said, "Man's nature is like swirling water. Open a passage for it to the east and it will flow to the east; open a passage to the west and it will flow to the west. Man's nature makes no distinction between east and west."

Mencius replied, "Water will indeed flow indifferently to east and west, but will it flow indifferently up or down? The tendency of man's nature to good is like the tendency of water to flow downhill . . . By striking water and causing it to leap up you make it go over your head, and by damming it and leading it you may force it uphill, but are such movements according to water's nature? No, it is the force applied which causes them. When men are made to do what is not good, their nature is subjected to force."

What is it that makes acting in accord with nature a good in and of itself? The Taoists, an early anti-intellectual movement in China, answered this kind of question with an apocryphal tale: The famous butcher of King Hui of Liang was so good that he never had to sharpen his knives. When asked the secret, he said, "When I get a new haunch of meat and it is ready to cut, I study it for a long while before I do anything. I picture how the animal looked with the flesh distributed on its bones, how its muscles worked when it was alive; how the ligaments functioned which connected the muscles to the bones. When I have studied the piece of meat so thoroughly that the pattern of the muscles, ligaments, and bones springs sharply into my mind, I raise my cleaver and strike the flesh. The pieces fall away like earth crumbling. Because my knife passes between the joints where there is nothing to cut, my blade is never dulled."

Lao Tzu, whose aphorisms face many of the pictures, spoke about the value of this kind of unforced action. Its value lay in its congruency with the way things were, not cutting against the grain but with it, moving effortlessly when the mind's eye tells you to use great force, yielding when you think resistance is called for, going low when your aspirations would take you high.

It is indeed water that sets an ideal example for human acts.

M.L.

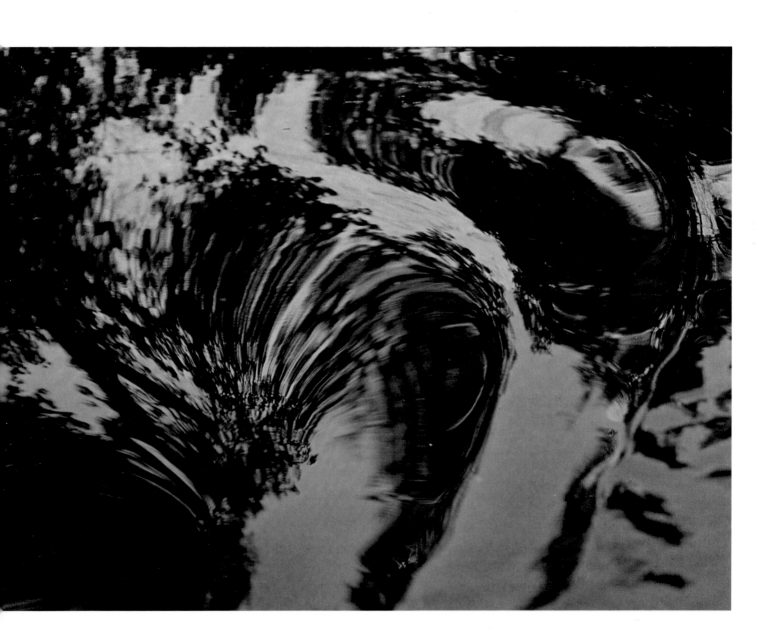

*That the yielding conquers the resistant and the soft conquers the hard
is a fact known by all men, yet utilized by none. . . .*

LAO TZU

Man at his best, like water,
Serves as he goes along;
Like water he seeks his own level,
The common level of life,
Loves living close to the earth,
Living clear down in his heart,
Loves kinship with his neighbors,
The pick of words that tell the truth,
The even tenor of the well loved state,
The fair profit of the able dealing,
The right timing of useful deeds,
And for blocking no one's way
No one blames him.

LAO TZU

A sage, in rambling about the Heights of Shang, saw a large and extraordinary tree.
The teams of a thousand chariots might be sheltered under it,
and its shade would cover them all! He said, "What a tree this is!
It must contain an extraordinary amount of timber!"

. . .

When he looked up, however, at its smaller branches,

they were so twisted and crooked that they could not be made into rafters and beams;

when he looked down to its root, its stem was divided into so many rounded portions

that neither coffin nor shell could be made from them.

He licked one of its leaves, and his mouth felt torn and wounded. The smell of it

would make a man frantic, as if intoxicated, for more than three whole days together.

"This, indeed," said he, "is a tree good for nothing,

and it is thus that it has reached so great an age."...

The cinnamon tree can be eaten, and therefore it is cut down.

The varnish tree is useful, and therefore incisions are made in it.

All men know the advantage of being useful,

but no one knows the advantage of being useless.

CHUANG TZU

The sage looks at the unity which belongs to all things,
and does not perceive where they have suffered loss.

CHUANG TZU

All within its circuit is preserved in peace,
and there comes to it no agitation from without.

CHUANG TZU

Nature may be compared to a vast ocean. Thousands and millions of changes are taking place in it. Crocodiles and fish are essentially of the same substance as the water in which they live. Man is crowded together with the myriad other things in the Great Changingness, and his nature is one with that of all other natural things. Knowing that I am of the same nature as all other natural things, I know that there is really no separate self, no separate personality, no absolute death and no absolute life.

T'IEN T'UNG-HSU
8TH CENTURY A.D.

There is a point of correspondency between two views which is called the pivot of the Tao. As soon as one finds this pivot, he stands in the center of the ring of thought where he can respond without end to the changing views; without end to those affirming, and without end to those denying.

CHUANG TZU

Death and life are looked on as but transformations;
the myriad creation is all of a kind,
there is a kinship through all.

HUAI NAN TZU
2D CENTURY B.C.

The essence of water is thick, viscous and congealed. It confers continuity of living, and not death. It gives rise to jade, turtles, dragons, the C'hing-chi *and the* Wei. *All are connected with water. People all drink water, but I alone take it as my model. People all have water, but I alone know how to make use of it. Why do we call water the preparative element? Because the myriad things get their life from it. So those who know on what water depends can know the true way in which water is preparatory to all things. People ask what water is. It is the* origin of all things, *and the ancestral temple of all Life. Water produces the beautiful and the ugly, the virtuous and the wicked, the foolish and the clever.*

AUTHOR UNKNOWN
5TH CENTURY B.C.

When water is still, its clearness shows the beard and eyebrows of him who looks into it. It is a perfect level, and the greatest artificer takes his rules from it. Such is the clearness of still water, and how much greater is that of the human Spirit! The still mind of the sage is the mirror of heaven and earth, the glass of all things.

CHUANG TZU

The people who live in villages bordering on the river lead its waters to irrigate their gardens, to which the water has no objection. The poor people disgusted with the filthy pools around drain them into the flowing river, but the foul water feels no exhilaration. Therefore, there is no difference whether the water is in the river or irrigating the garden; it is a matter of indifference to the water whether it lies in the filthy pool or in the flowing Chiang. Therefore the sage rests satisfied with his position, whether high or low, and joyfully follows his work and avocation of sage.

HUAI NAN TZU

In the subterranean regions there are alternate layers of earth and rock and flowing spring waters. These strata rest upon thousands of vapours (ch'i) which are distributed in tens of thousands of branches, veins and thread-like openings. The veins are slanting and delicate, like axles interlocking and communicating. It is like a machine rotating in the depths, and the circulation takes place as if the veins had intimate mutual connections and as if there were piston bellows at work. The mysterious network (hsuan kang) spreads out and joins together every part of the roots of the earth. The innermost parts of the earth are neither metal nor stone nor earth nor water as we know them. Thousands and ten thousands of horizontal and vertical veins like warp and weft weave together in mutual embrace. Millions of miles of earth are as if hanging and floating on a sea boundlessly vast. Taking all including land and sea as earth, the secret and mystery is that the roots communicate with each other. The natures, veins, colours, tastes and sounds, both of the earth, the waters, and the stones, differ from place to place. So also the animals, birds, herbs, trees and all natural products, have different shapes and natures in different places.

Now if the ch'i of the earth tich'i can get through the veins, then the water and the earth above will be fragrant and flourishing . . . and all men and things will be pure and wise. . . . But if the ch'i of the earth is stopped up, then the water and earth and natural products [above] will be bitter, cold and withered . . . and all men and things will be evil and foolish. . . .

The body of the earth is like that of a human being. In men there is much heat in and under the watery abdominal organs; if this were not so, they could not digest their food nor do their work. So also the earth below the aqueous region is extremely hot; if this were not so, it could not "shrink" all the waters [i.e., evaporate them and leave mineral deposits], and it could not drive off all the [aqueous] Yin ch'i. *Ordinary people, not being able to see the veins and vessels which are disposed in order within the body of man, think that it is no more than a lump of solid flesh. Likewise, not being able to see the veins and vessels which are disposed in order under the ground, they think that the earth is just a homogeneous mass. They do not realise that heaven, earth, human beings, and natural things, all have their dispositions and organisations. Even a thread of smoke, a broken bit of ice, a tumbledown wall of an old tile, all have their dispositions and organisations. How can anyone say that the earth does not have its dispositions and organisations?*

CHENG SSU-HSIAO
1206-1283 A.D.

. . . a sound man is good at salvage,
at seeing that nothing is lost . . .
LAO TZU

Here is the ditch of dead and hopeless water;
No breeze can raise a ripple on it.
Best to throw in it scraps of rusty iron and copper,
Pour out in it all the refuse of meat and soup.

Perhaps the copper will turn green like emeralds,
Perhaps the rusty iron will assume the shape of peach blossoms;
Let grass weave a layer of silky gauze
And bacteria puff up patches of cloud and haze.

So let the dead water ferment into green wine,
Littered with floating pearls of white foam.
Small pearls cackle aloud and become big pearls,
Only to be burst like gnats and to rob the vintage.

So this ditch of dead and hopeless water
May boast a touch of brightness.
If the toads cannot endure the deathly silence,
The water may burst out singing.

Here is a ditch of dead and hopeless water,
A region where beauty can never stay.
Better abandon it to evil—
Then, perhaps, some beauty will come of it.

WEN I-TUO
1899-1946

The clouds of sunset
Gather in the western sky,
And over the silent silvery Han
Rises a white jade moon.

Not often does life
Bring such beauty.

Where shall I see the moon
Next year?

SU T'UNG-PO
1037-1101 A.D.

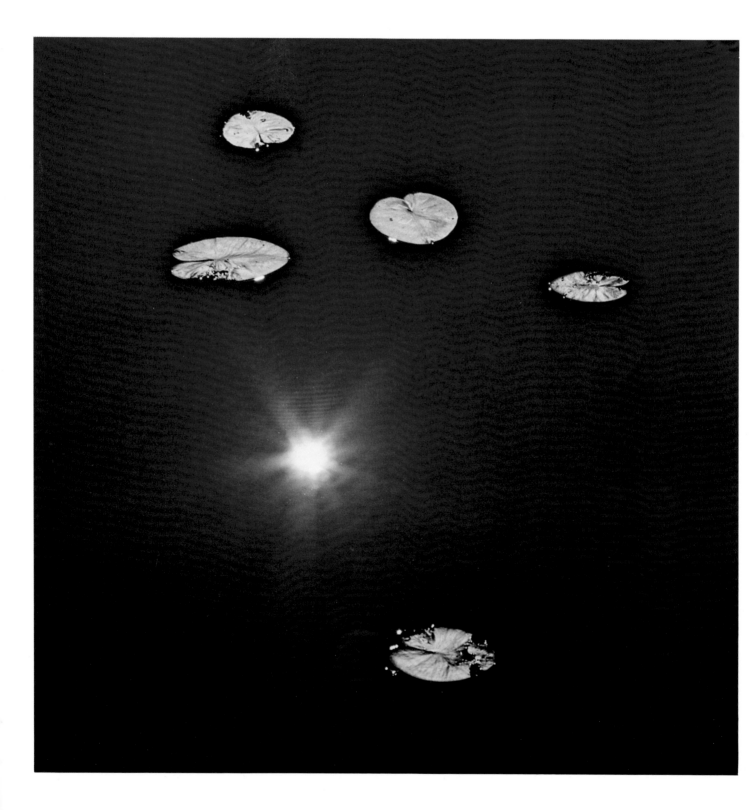

Moon-gazing;
    Looking at it, it clouds over;
        Not looking, it becomes clear.
            CHORA
            1729-1781 A.D.

Taking up one blade of grass,
Use it as a sixteen-foot Buddha

AUTHOR UNKNOWN

Morning haze;
*   as in a painting of a dream—*
*   men go their ways.*
                    BUSON
                1715-1783 A.D.

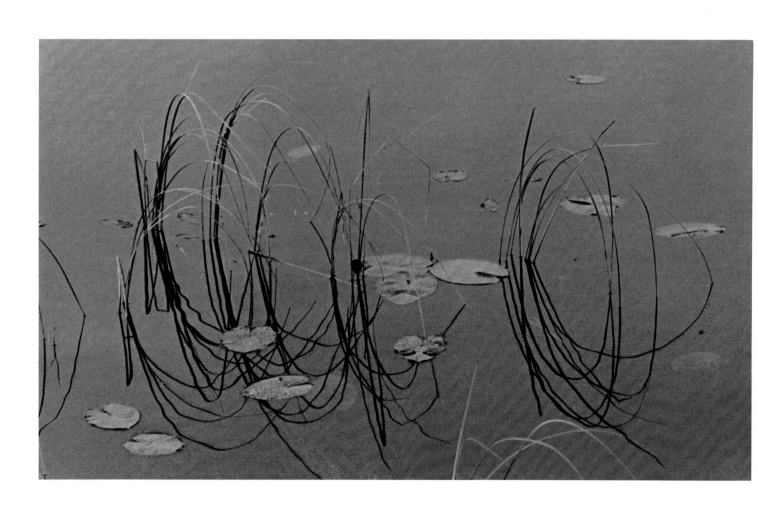

High noon;
save for reed sparrows,
the river makes no sound.

ISSA
1763-1828 A.D.

Wind passes over the lake.
The swelling waves stretch away
Without limit. Autumn comes with the twilight,
And boats grow rare on the river.
Flickering waters and fading mountains
Always touch the heart of man.
I never grow tired of singing
Of their boundless beauty.
The lotus pods are already formed,
And the water lilies have grown old.
The dew has brightened the blossoms
Of the arrowroot along the riverbank.
The herons and seagulls sleep
On the sand with their
Heads tucked away, as though
They did not wish to see
The men who pass by on the river.

LI CH'ING-CHAO
1081-1143 A.D.

All the long night
The rain pattered down
On the thick, thatched eaves
Of my hut.

This night, on ten times
Ten thousand farms,
It has stirred the rice seed
To new life.

When the warm sun comes up,
I shoulder my hoe
And go blithely forth
To my field,

And I sing a song as I go,
Of the blue, blue sky,
And the water that shines
So green.

TSE NAN
CH'ING DYNASTY, 1644-1911 A.D.

I sit through the long night
In the high tower,
And listen to the autumn rain
Outside my window.

There is no sound of human life,
Save now and then
A belated traveler hastening by.
Through the dark heavens
A wild goose
Wings his lonely flight.
In the chill gloom
A cricket calls.
The water drips mournfully
From the t'ung trees,
And the blossoms
Flutter sadly
To the rain-soaked earth.

Sadness broods
Over the world.

CH'ENG WANG
CH'ING DYNASTY, 1644-1911 A.D.

The rain drips and drips!
The hour strikes and strikes!
Outside the window the plantain, inside the window the lamp,
At such a time the feelings are unbounded.

Dreams hard to fashion!
Regrets hard to smooth out!
No wonder a sorrower mislikes to hear:
In the empty courtyard the dripping lasts till dawn.

MO CH'I-YUNG
11TH-12TH CENTURY A.D.

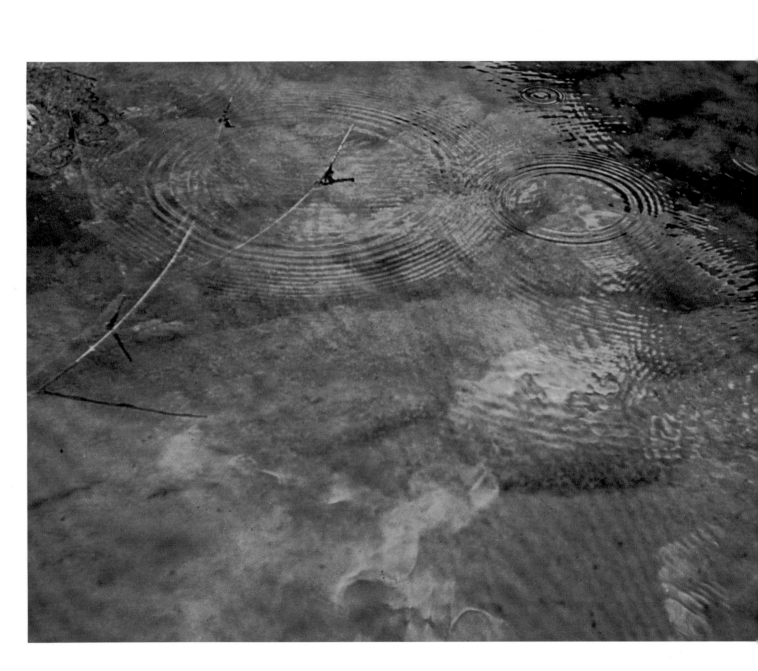

Unafraid of the dashing rain on the pool,
Enamelled leaves conceal each other.
Colorful birds suddenly fly in alarm,
Their rush scatters the sunset glow on the ripples.

MEI YAO-CHIEN
1002-1060 A.D.

Do you not see
That you and I
Are as the branches
Of one tree?
With your rejoicing
Comes my laughter;
With your sadness
Start my tears.
Love,
Could life be otherwise
With you and me?

TZU YEH
TSIN DYNASTY, 265-316 A.D.

How swift was your departure,
How slow your coming home!
Let's drink deeply of the good warm wine,
And drown the years between!

SU CH'AN-I
SUI DYNASTY, 589-618 A.D.

All the rains of June;
* and one evening, secretly*
* through the*
* pines—the moon.*

RYOTA
1707-1787 A.D.

I have sailed the River of Yellow Flowers,
Borne by the channel of a green stream,
Rounding ten thousand turns through the mountains
On a journey of less than thirty miles . . .
. . . where light grows dim in the thick pines,
The surface of an inlet sways with nut-horns
And weeds are lush along the banks.
. . . Down in my heart I have always been as pure
As this limpid water is. . . .

WANG WEI
699-759 A.D.

Young man,
Seize every minute
Of your time.
The days fly by;
Ere long you too
Will grow old.

If you believe me not,
See there, in the courtyard,
How the frost
Glitters white and cold and cruel
On the grass
That once was green.

TZU YEH
TSIN DYNASTY, 265-316 A.D.

All the scenery in the north
Is enclosed in a thousand li of ice,
And ten thousand li of whirling snow.
Behold both sides of the Great Wall—
There is only a vast confusion left.
On the upper and lower reaches of the Yellow River
You can no longer see the flowing water.
The mountains are dancing silver serpents,
The hills on the plains are shining elephants.
I desire to compare our height with the skies.
In clear weather
The earth is so charming,
Like a red-faced girl clothed in white.
Such is the charm of these rivers and mountains,
Calling innumerable heroes to vie with each other in pursuing her. . . .

MAO TSE-TUNG
1893-

With you I wandered down the Nine Rivers;
A whirlwind rose and the waters barred us with their waves.
We rode in a water-chariot with awning of lotus-leaf
Drawn by two dragons, with griffins to pull at the sides.
I climb K'un-lun and look in all directions;
My heart rises all a-flutter, I am agitated and distraught.
Dusk is coming, but I am too sad to think of return.
Of the far shore only are my thoughts; I lie awake and yearn.

In his fish-scale house, dragon-scale hall,
Portico of purple-shell, in his red palace,
What is the Spirit doing, down in the water?
Riding a white turtle, followed by stripy fish
With you I wandered in the islands of the River.
The ice is on the move; soon the floods will be down.
You salute me with raised hands, then go towards the East.
I go with my lovely one as far as the southern shore.
The waves surge on surge come to meet him,
Fishes shoal after shoal escort me on my homeward way.

AUTHOR UNKNOWN

C. 400 B.C.

The cottage goes round the curved creek;
Bamboos follow the bend of the mountain.
Streams and mountains are still there
In the midst of white clouds.
Come to the creek and free the skiff;
Sit here with your back to the mountain.
With the river birds and mountain flowers,
Share my leisure.

WANG AN-SHIH
1021–1086 A.D.

Seafarers tell of the Isles of Ying,

shadowy in spindrift and waves, truly hard to seek out;

Yüeh men describe T'ien-mu,

in clouds and rainbows clear or shrouded, there for eyes to glimpse;

T'ien-mu touching the sky, surging toward the sky,

lord above the Five Peaks, shadowing the Red Wall;

T'ien-t'ai's forty-eight thousand fathoms

beside it seem to topple and sprawl to south and east.

I longed, and my longing became a dream of Wu-Yueh;

in the night I flew across the moon of Mirror Lake;

the lake moon, lighting my shadow,

saw me to the Valley of Shan,

Lord Hsieh's old home there today,

where green waters rush and roll and shrill monkeys cry.

Feet thrust into Lord Hsieh's clogs,

body climbing ladders of blue cloud,

halfway up the scraps I see the ocean sun,

and in the air hear the cocks of heaven.

A thousand cliffs, ten thousand clefts, trails uncertain,

I turn aside for flowers, rest on rocks—suddenly it's night;

bear growls, dragon purrs in the din of cliffside torrents

shake the deep forest, startle the piled-up peaks;

clouds blue-dark, threatening rain,

waters soft-seething, sending up mists;

a rent of lightning, crack of thunder,

and hilltops sunder and fall;

doors of stone at grotto mouths

swing inward with a grinding roar,

and from the blue darkness, bottomless, vast and wild,

sun and moon shine sparkling on terraces of silver and gold.

Rainbows for robes, wind for horses,
whirling whirling, the Lord of the Clouds comes down,
tigers twanging zithers, luan birds to turn his carriage,
and immortal men in files thick as hemp—
 Suddenly my soul shudders, my spirit leaps,
 in terror I rise up with repeated sighs;
 only the mat and pillow where now I woke—
 lost are the mists of a moment ago!
All the joys of the world are like this,
the many-evented past a river flowing east.
I leave you now—when will I return?—
to loose the white deer among green bluffs,
in my wandering to ride them in search of famed hills.
How can I knit brows, bend back to serve influence and power,
never dare to wear an open-hearted face?

LI PO
701-762 A.D.

For ten miles the mountains rise
Above the lake. The beauty
Of water and mountain is
Impossible to describe.
In the glow of evening
A traveller sits in front
Of an inn, sipping wine.
The moon shines above a
Little bridge and a single
Fisherman. Around the farm
A bamboo fence descends to
The water. I chat with an
Old man about work and crops.
Maybe, when the years have come
When I can lay aside my
Cap and robe of office,
I can take a little boat
And come back to this place.

CHU HSI
1130-1200 A.D.

For long have I cherished the desire to enjoy the gloom;

Today I have freedom to explore.

The Yangtze joins the lands of Ch'u and Shu,

A thousand branches flow south and east.

Ho River strikes like lightning,

Green waves of Ch'ien turn blue.

Other currents are far too many;

From afar they come rushing together.

Entering the gorge roads disappear;

Interlocked mountains are like a shrine.

Winding around they tower in this vast water,

Shrinking an abyss into a pool. . . .

Wind sound like breath, clouds rise like spittle.

Hanging cliffs whisper, dangling creepers are fresh and green.

Cliff bamboos look cold and blue, a lonesome stone-cedar grows.

Spray flies like tumbling snow, strange stones shaped like alarmed horses.

To cross these streams one must know their depth;

Some boys suddenly appear gathering wood for fuel.

By chance appear some human dwellings;

On the sand bank you can get a sedan chair.

By seven in the evening the region is deserted;

The local lord is an old-fashioned moralist.

The yamen closes its doors when the evening drum sounds.

Guests are entertained with frozen oranges.

I have heard that here grows the Huang-ching grass;

Green-jade bamboos flourish.

I eat and drink my fill

But no P'eng or Tan appears.

Climate is mild here in winter,

Milky Way stays half submerged at night.

. . .

Old loyalists still mourn for Ch'ang and Yen,

It is an old custom to accept fish and silkworms as gifts.

Houses are made of boards but use no tiles,

Hillside huts are narrow like monasteries.

To go out and cut firewood is an adventure here;

Never does one get a full pot of rice.

Pity, what a poor life!

They work hard and are not ashamed.

This leaf of a boat lightly travels far;

It is strong against big waves.

Terror melts away, we look at each other with a vacant stare;

They utter something but we cannot converse.

How can one live in such wild and barren lands?

It is difficult to take delight in this dark gloom.

I only like that lonely pigeon-hawk resting

A hundred feet above the mountain mist.

It flies across with great poise,

It flies far, seemingly without effort.

Wings flapping, it flies towards the Milky Way,

Caring not for sparrows or quails.

This is a sick world of dust and toil,

Restraints I face are unbearable.

To dwell in complete retirement like a recluse,

How wonderful that would be!

But we are all drunk with worldly desires.

I watch the joy of a flying bird,

Hiding my desires behind lofty ideals.

Su T'ung-po

I climb the road to Cold Mountain,
the road to Cold Mountain that never ends.
The valleys are long and strewn with boulders,
the streams broad and banked with thick grass.
Moss is slippery though no rain has fallen;
pines sigh but it isn't the wind.
Who can break from the snares of the world.
and sit with me among the white clouds?

Cold Mountain is full of weird sights;
people who try to climb it always get scared.
When the moon shines, the water glints and sparkles;
when the wind blows, the grasses rustle and sigh.
Snowflakes make blossoms for the bare plum,
clouds in place of leaves for the naked trees.
At a touch of rain the whole mountain shimmers—
but only in good weather can you make the climb. . . .

Among a thousand clouds and ten thousand streams
here lives an idle man,
in the daytime wandering over green mountains,
at night coming home to sleep by the cliff.
Swiftly the springs and autumns pass,
but my mind is at peace, free of dust and delusion.
How pleasant, to know I need nothing to lean on,
to be still as the waters of the autumn river!

HAN SHAN
8TH CENTURY A.D.

When moods come I follow them alone,
to no purpose learning fine things for myself,
going till I come to where the river ends,
sitting and watching when clouds rise up.
By chance I meet an old man of the woods;
we talk and laugh—we have no "going-home" time.
WANG WEI

The water murmurs
In the old stone well,
And, a rippling mirror,
Gives back the clear blue sky.
The river roars,
Swollen with the late rains of spring.
On the cool, jade-green grass
The golden sunshine
Splashes.

Sometimes, at early dawn,
I climb
Even as far as Lien Shan Temple.
In the spring
I plow the thirsty field,
That it may drink new life.
I eat a little,
I work a little.
Each day my hair grows thinner,
And, it seems,
I lean ever a bit more heavily
On my old thornwood cane.

LIU TZU-HUI
SUNG DYNASTY, 960-1278 A.D.

The two old men
Sit in silence together,
Living in dim memories
Of the past.
They are lifelong friends
And need no words
To share their thoughts.

One quavers to the other;
"May you live a hundred years,
And may I live ninety-nine."

The other nods his old white head
And gravely says;
"Let us go home together
And drink a cup of wine."

HSU CHI
SUNG DYNASTY, 960-1278 A.D.

The day is done.
Back to their folds
Come ox and sheep.

Just as the drum
Beats the sunset hour,
I reach the shore.
Swift on the stream
Creep the mist and the dark.
To my ear comes the thud
Of a passing oar.
A great fish leaps
In sudden fear.
Dimly seen,
A ghostly sail flits by.

The wind from the north
Sweeps down on the world.
The night is come.

CH'EN FU
YUAN DYNASTY, 1260-1341 A.D.

High and lofty, tiers of rock,
How solitary they stand.
Luckily, in this strong wind the green bamboos cluster;
Sun sets, no one about, seagulls have left.
Only the distant water remains,
Keeping company with the cold reeds.

SU T'UNG-PO

A hawk hovers in air.
Two white gulls float on the stream.
Soaring with the wind, it is easy
To drop and seize
Birds who foolishly drift with the current.
Where the dew sparkles in the grass,
The spider's web waits for its prey.
The processes of nature resemble the business of men.
I stand alone with ten thousand sorrows.

TU FU

. . . I love this decaying autumn.

Yellow leaves tumble in wind and rain,
Spots of white sway over rivers and lakes.
You cannot get to those lakes and rivers;
It is hard labor to transplant trees.
Silently a pair of wild ducks come flying;
All this becomes a painting.

SU T'UNG-PO

Where the lotus pool
Is fragrant with its flowers,
We drank our last farewell
From cups of jade.

You thought I shunned you
When I, quickly turning,
Hid my face from you,
And would not look again.

Ah!
Being but a man,
How could you know, belovèd,
That it was to wipe
The scalding tears away?

HUANG PIEN
T'ANG DYNASTY, 618-905 A.D.

The setting sun
Shines on the village
At the river's mouth,
And the spring wind
Softly stirs
The snow-white blossoms
On the bank.

We've said
Our last farewells,
And now
You're floating
Down the stream.

Why does the twilight
Come so fast?—
Or is it the mist?
For I scarce can see
Your figure
In the fast-receding
Boat.

HAN HUNG
T'ANG DYNASTY, 618-905 A.D.

A flower,
A willow,
A fisherman
On a rock.

A ray of sun
On the river,
A bird
On the wing.

Halfway
Up the mountain
A priest slowly climbs
To a shrine.

In the forest
A yellow leaf
Flutters and falls.

HO P'EI-YU
CH'ING DYNASTY, 1644-1911 A.D.

The River flows to the East.
Its waves have washed away all
The heroes of history.
To the West of the ancient
Wall you enter the Red Gorge
Of Chu Ko Liang of the
Days of the Three Kingdoms. The
Jagged peaks pierce the heavens.
The furious rapids beat
At the boat, and dash up in
A thousand clouds of spray like
Snow. Mountain and river have
Often been painted, in the
Memory of the heroes
Of those days. I remember
Long ago, Kung Ch'in newly
Married to the beautiful
Chiao-hsiao, shining in splendor,
A young warrior, and the other
Chu Ko Liang, in his blue cap,
Waving his horsetail duster,
Smiling and chatting as he
Burned the navy of Ts'ao Ts'ao.
Their ashes were scattered to
The four winds. They vanished away
In smoke. I like to dream of
Those dead kingdoms. Let people
Laugh at my prematurely
Grey hair. My answer is
A wine cup, full of the
Moon drowned in the River.

SU T'UNG-PO

. . . since water still flows, though we cut it with our swords
And sorrow returns, though we drown it with wine,
Since the world can in no way answer to our craving,
I will loosen my hair tomorrow and take to a fishing-boat.

LI PO

China is vague and immense where the nine rivers pour.
The horizon is a deep line threading north and south.
Blue haze and rain.
Hills like a snake or tortoise guard the river.

The yellow crane is gone.
  Where?
Now this tower and region are for the wanderer.
I drink wine to the bubbling water—the heroes are gone.
Like a tidal wave a wonder rises in my heart.

MAO TSE-TUNG

To what can we liken human life?
Perhaps to a wild swan's footprints on mud or snow;
Before it flies off at random, east or west . . .

HSIN CH'I-CH'I
1140-1207 A.D.

When he is born, man is soft and weak; in death he becomes stiff and hard.
The ten thousand creatures and all plants and trees while they are alive
are supple and soft, but when they are dead they become brittle and dry.
Truly, what is stiff and hard is a "companion of death";
what is soft and weak is a "companion of life."
Therefore "the weapon that is too hard will be broken,
the tree that has the hardest wood will be cut down."

. . .

Truly, the hard and mighty are cast down;
the soft and weak set on high.
LAO TZU

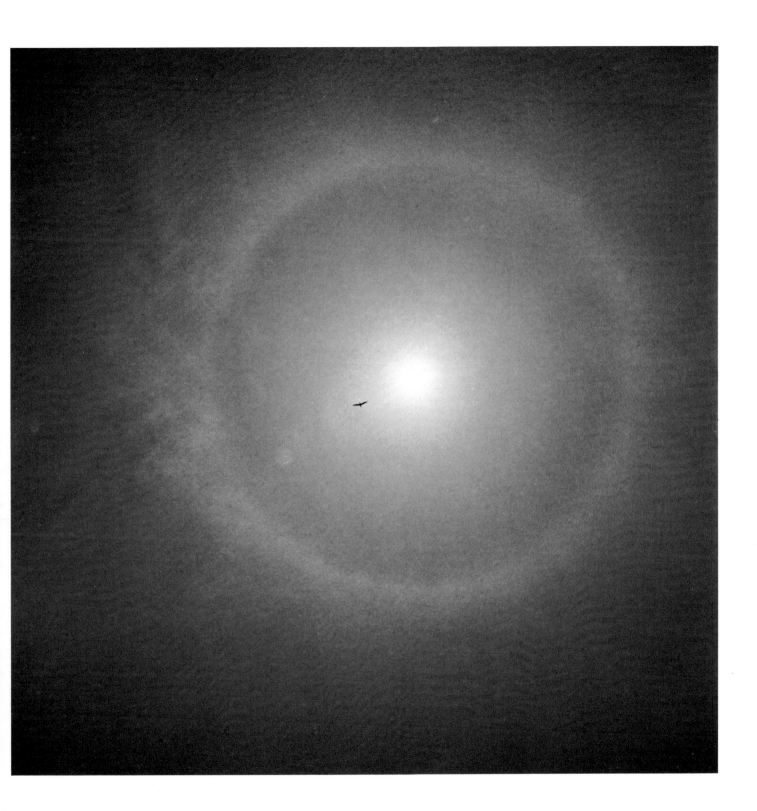

Acknowledgments

WE ARE GRATEFUL for the Chinese cultural tradition. Many more people have lived under it than under Europe's, and it is at least a thousand years older even if we trace Europe's to the Greece of Homer and the Hebraism of Moses. Henry H. Hart points this out to us in his book, *The Hundred Names,* the title poem of which appears on page 60. The farmer of "The Hundred Names," Mr. Hart tells us, "is the farmer of *The Good Earth,*" his song "expressive of the mind of the Chinese farmer today [1933]."

We are grateful to the poets and poetesses and to the translators who have let us know what was meant, however Procrustean the bed the poems had to fit. Mr. Hart describes his own method: "The poem is carefully studied in the original. The text is restored to its original form as far as possible. A rough literal translation is then made, the meanings of each word and phrase being noted. After a few readings of this translation, the words and phrases fall into a pattern which, to the translator, appear to convey the proper meaning of the poem. The words and their meanings thus approximate the Chinese syllables and their connotations, as far as the differences in the two languages permit. . . . The translator must divorce himself from the Western response to experience."

I met Mr. Hart briefly in the early 'forties, when he was trying to persuade the University of California Press, where I was then an editor, to keep *The Hundred Names* in print, and it is a pleasure to know that a facsimile of the book, titled *Poems from the Hundred Names,* was published in 1968 by The Greenwood Press. I have enjoyed his introductory material deeply, and must borrow from it further:

"Finally, the most fascinating and interesting problem of translation is the interpretation of the ideograph. Every Chinese syllable presents two problems. The first, comparatively simple, is the translation of the syllable by that English word or phrase which most nearly approximates it; the second is the study of the suggested potentialities of the ideograph. The poet often drives home his thought, and at the same time expresses an implication or a variation of emotional response, within the strokes of a single character. This may require several English words, a phrase, or even an entire sentence for its adequate elucidation. It must be kept constantly in mind that Chinese writing is, in the first analysis, a series of pictures of ideas. Inflections, tenses, articles, auxiliaries—most of these are lacking in the language, and must be supplied. . . .

"These, then, are the problems of the translator in a field which has been far from overcrowded. Thousands of beautiful lyrics still await translation, and every one that is given to us brings us closer to a real comprehension of the Chinese mind and spirit. More than this, each translation brings to our own culture an added richness, warmth, color, and depth."

We thank Mr. Hart for his work with words and ideographs. We thank Marc Lappé, who dropped almost everything when we showed him four albums of mounted McCurdy prints and he renewed his old delights with his search of Oriental literature for the selections here. We thank Werner Linz, then of McGraw-Hill, who knew at a glance that those albums contained our third book in this series, and Fred Hills, now of McGraw-Hill, for agreeing. We thank John McCurdy for proving this not quite so, flying to London from Uppsala with new photographs and old, and working all through a day and a night there to blend in the new material. We thank Philip H. Evans for sharing that day and night, adding his own photographic expertise there and, again and again, in Verona. We thank Roberto Voltolina, of Mondadori Editore, who translates Mr. Evans's Welsh-flavored English into fluent Italian presswork.

Thus we thank the Welsh, British, and Italians for what they have enabled Friends of the Earth in the United States to draw from Chinese literature to grace the work of a Korean man with a Scottish name who has been teaching photography in Sweden and photographing so well almost everywhere. Kenneth Brower, David Gancher, Betty Lynn Moulton, and Ann McConnell have assisted in the selections, and have added Japan and a touch of Sufi. We thank all whose translations we have used.

Most of all, we are grateful for the richness the earth's great diversity of cultures has produced.   D.R.B.

*Such is the nature of the ocean that
the waters which flow into it can never fill it,
nor those which flow from it exhaust it.*

CHUANG TZU
369-286 B.C.

SOURCES

(To be considered as part of copyright notice, page 12.)

Barnstone, Willis. *The Poems of Mao Tse-tung,* © 1972, Bantam Books, Inc., New York.

Blofeld, John. *The Wheel of Life,* © 1972, Shambala Press, Berkeley, California.

Blyth, R. H. *Haiku,* Volume I: *Eastern Culture,* © 1945 by R. H. Blyth, The Hokuserdo Press, Tokyo.

Bynner, Witter and Kang-hu, Kiang. *The Jade Mountain,* © 1929, Alfred A. Knopf, Inc., New York.

Bynner, Witter. *The Way of Life,* © 1962, Capricorn Books, New York.

Engle, Hua-ling and Engle, Paul. *The Poems of Mao Tse-tung,* © 1972, Dell Paperbacks, New York.

Hart, Henry H. *The Hundred Names,* © 1933 by The Regents of the University of California, University of California Press, Berkeley, California. (Facsimile edition, 1968, The Greenwood Press, Westport, Conn.)

Henderson, Harold G. *An Introduction to Haiku,* © 1958 by H. G. Henderson, Doubleday and Co., Garden City, New York.

Kotewall, Robert and Smith, Norman L. *The Penguin Book of Chinese Verse,* © 1962, by N. L. Smith and R. Kotewall, Penguin Books, Inc., Baltimore, Maryland.

Legge, James. *The Texts of Taoism,* © 1959, Julian Press, New York.

Legge, James. *The Works of Mencius,* © 1970, Dover Books, Inc., New York.

Liu, James J. Y. *The Art of Chinese Poetry,* © 1962 by J. J. Y. Liu,

University of Chicago Press, Chicago, Illinois.

Needham, Joseph. *Science and Civilisation in China, Volume I,* First edition, © 1954, Cambridge University Press, New York.

Payne, Robert. *The White Pony, An Anthology of Chinese Poetry,* © 1947, by John Day Co., Mentor Books, New York.

Reps, Paul. *Zen Flesh, Zen Bones,* © 1961, Anchor Books, Garden City, New York.

Rexroth, Kenneth. *One Hundred Poems from the Chinese,* © 1971, New Directions Publishing Co., New York.

Tagore, Amitendranath. *Moments of Rising Mist, A Collection of S'ung Landscape Poetry,* © 1973, Grossman Publishers, Inc., New York.

Van Over, Raymond. *Chinese Mysticism,* © 1972, Harper & Row, New York.

Veith, Ilza. *The Yellow Emperor's Classic of Internal Medicine;* © 1966, University of California Press, Berkeley, California.

Waley, Arthur. *The Nine Songs: A Study in Shamanism in Ancient China,* © 1955, George Allen and Unwin, Ltd., London.

Waley, Arthur. *The Way and Its Power,* © 1958, Grove Press, Inc., New York.

Watson, Burton. *Chinese Lyricism: Shih Poetry from the Second to the Twelfth Century,* © 1971, Columbia University Press, New York.

Wilhelm, Richard and Baynes, Cary. *The I Ching,* © 1950, Princeton University Press, Princeton, New Jersey.

Publisher's note: This book is set in Centaur and Arrighi by Mackenzie & Harris, Inc., San Francisco. Color separations, lithography, and binding are by Arnoldo Mondadori Editore, Verona, on coated paper made by Cartiera Celdit and double-page collated and bound in Coloreta of Scholco. Lay out is by Marc Lappé. Design is by David R. Brower.